WILD KRATTS™

Go, Creature Powers!

By Martin Kratt and Chris Kratt

A Random House PICTUREBACK® Book

Random House 🏠 New York

randomhousekids.com
ISBN 978-1-101-93306-0 (pbk.) — ISBN 978-1-101-93307-7 (ebook)
MANUFACTURED IN CHINA
10 9 8 7 6 5 4

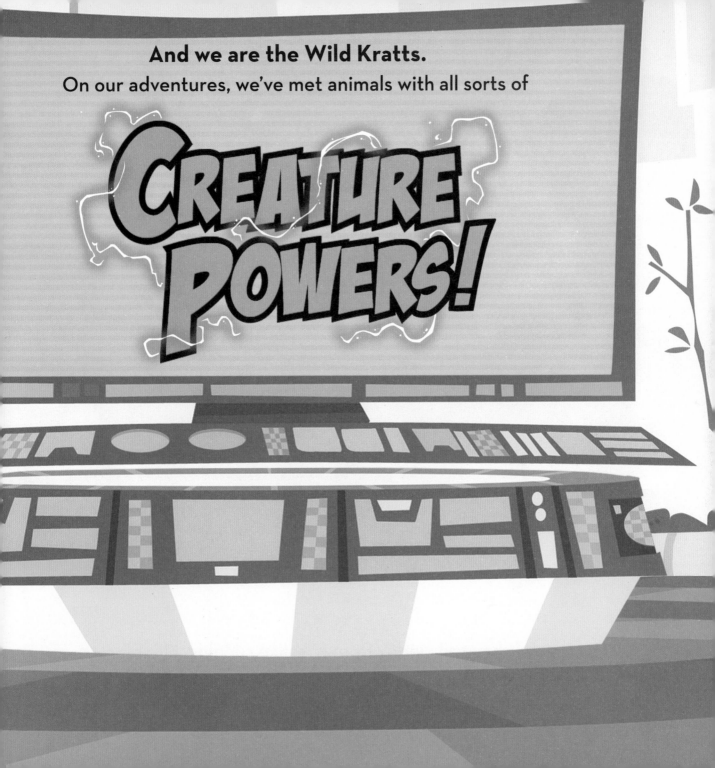

And we are the Wild Kratts.
On our adventures, we've met animals with all sorts of

CREATURE POWERS!

Animals have all kinds of powers, like running, climbing, swimming, and flying.
But what is the most powerful Creature Power of all?

CHARGING POWER!

Rhinos have three tons of muscle covered by a thick skin that looks like armor. They have very tough horns on their noses. Rhinos are strong, fast, and famous for charging.

A charging rhino is so strong it can flip a truck!

TRUNK POWER!

Elephants are the heaviest and strongest land animal on planet Earth!

Elephants have powerful muscles in their noses. An elephant's nose, also called a trunk, can pick up a person. And an elephant is so strong it can push over big trees!

But strength isn't the only power. What about flying? Elephants don't fly.

FLYING POWER!

Peregrine falcons are the fastest fliers on the planet. When this falcon dives or stoops, it can hit speeds of over 200 miles per hour.

To fly so fast, a peregrine falcon needs some extra features. Special see-through eyelids protect its eyes like goggles. And channels in its nostrils slow the fast-moving air flowing into its nose. This helps the falcon breathe.

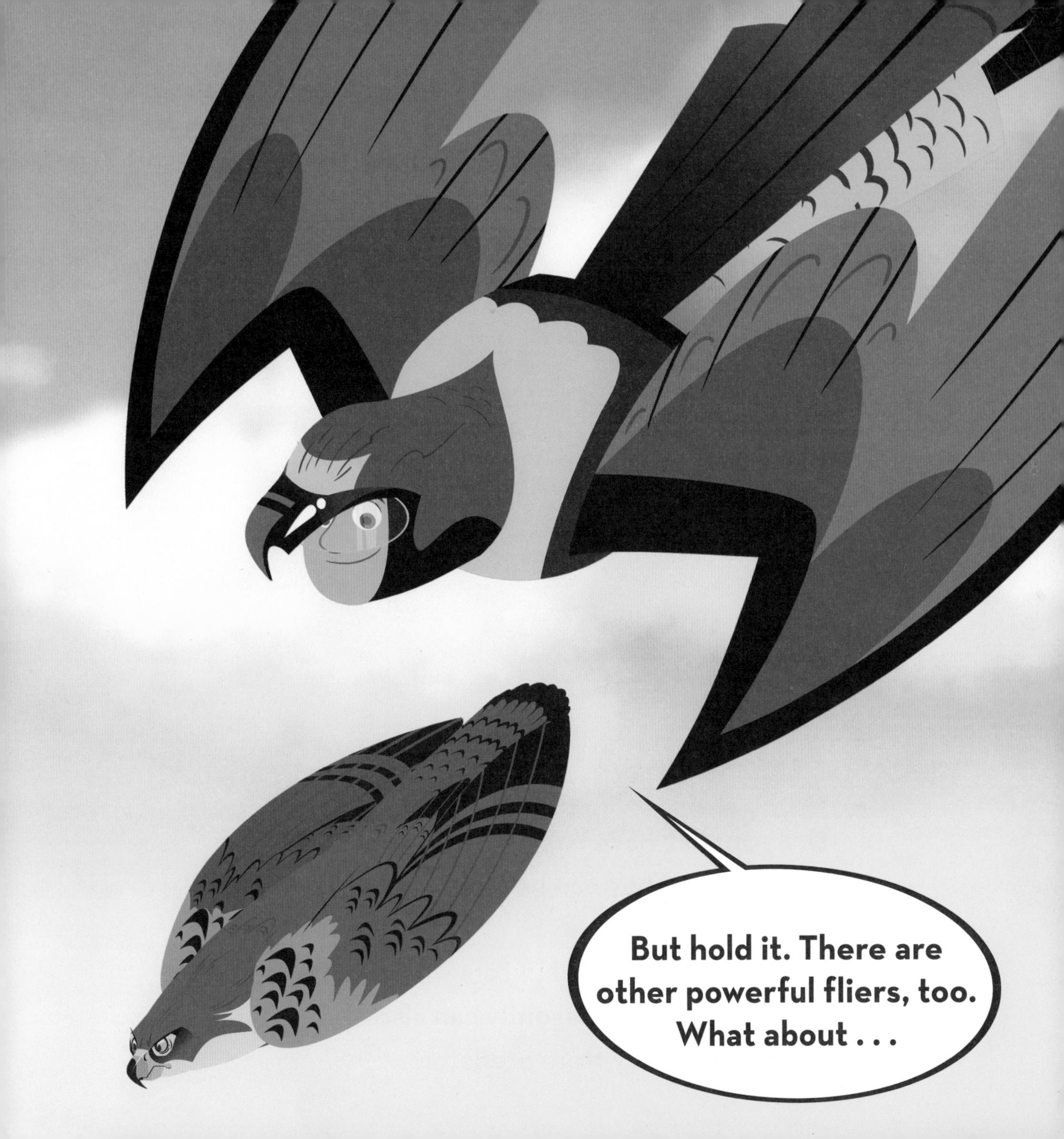
But hold it. There are other powerful fliers, too. What about . . .

HOVER POWER!

Dragonflies have been flying since the days of the dinosaurs. They can hover and fly backward and upside down.

Dragonflies are swift hunters who catch other insects in the air. A dragonfly can also use its flying powers to get away from predators.

BIG BITE POWER!

Hippos can open their mouths extremely wide. A male hippo has teeth over one and a half feet long! **Nile crocodiles** have over sixty teeth in their mouths. And they have very powerful bites when their jaws chomp down.

These creatures are two of the biggest biters at the watering hole!

Don't forget the big biters in the ocean. How about . . .

. . . **SHARKS!** These are some powerful biters.

Great white sharks have serrated teeth for tearing and ripping!

Tiger sharks have bites powerful enough to cut through sea turtle shells.

And both **bull sharks** and tiger sharks will bite and try to eat anything they can catch.

However, other swimmers can escape with . . .

SWIMMING POWER!

Dolphins can swim faster than sharks. Dolphins can also leap out of the water to get away.

Sea otters are swimmers who can twist and turn and hide in giant seaweed called kelp.

Sharks don't mess with **orcas**. These big cousins of the dolphin can eat those big sharks!

Well, I'm the swimming brother, and I say this is the most powerful Creature Power.

But not in a tree! This climbing brother prefers . . .

CLIMBING POWER!

Orangutans climb all the time. They are arboreal. That means they live in trees. Orangutans are the heaviest arboreal animals in the world.

Spider monkeys don't have thumbs, so their hands act as hooks. This makes them expert swingers. Plus, they have prehensile tails. That means their tails can grab and be used for climbing.

Geckos are little lizards that are great climbers. Their feet and toes create a charge of static electricity that helps them cling to all kinds of surfaces!

Climbing, swimming, and . . .

running!

RUNNING POWER!

Cheetahs run over seventy miles per hour. That's as fast as cars on a superhighway. Cheetahs are the undisputed fastest sprinters on Earth!

A cheetah has claws that dig into the dirt for traction and long legs that stretch out for big strides.

STINK POWER!

A **skunk** is an amazing animal that can do handstands and shoot a super stink to defend itself. One squirt of that stink, and almost any creature will leave the skunk alone!

Okay, skunk, you win! You have today's most powerful Creature Power!

Go, Creature Powers!